GIVE & TAKE

Fabric Appliqué

Daphne Greig &
Susan Purney Mark

Located in Paducah, Kentucky, the American Quilter's Society (AQS) is dedicated to promoting the accomplishments of today's quilters. Through its publications and events, AQS strives to honor today's quiltmakers and their work and to inspire future creativity and innovation in quiltmaking.

EXECUTIVE BOOK EDITOR: ANDI MILAM REYNOLDS
SENIOR EDITOR: LINDA BAXTER LASCO
COPY EDITOR: CHRYSTAL ABHALTER
GRAPHIC DESIGN: MELISSA POTTERBAUM
COVER DESIGN: MICHAEL BUCKINGHAM
PHOTOGRAPHY: CHARLES R. LYNCH

Additional copies of this book may be ordered from the American Quilter's Society, PO Box 3290, Paducah, KY 42002-3290, or online at www.AmericanQuilter.com.

Text © 2011, Author, Daphne Greig & Susan Purney Mark
Artwork © 2011, American Quilter's Society

LIBRARY OF CONGRESS CATALOGING-IN-PUBLICATION DATA

Greig, Daphne.
  Give & take fabric appliqué / by Daphne Greig and Susan Purney Mark.
     p. cm.
  ISBN 978-1-60460-005-6
  1. Machine appliqué--Patterns. 2. Machine quilting--Patterns.
I. Mark,
Susan Purney. II. Title. III. Title: Give and take fabric appliqué.
  TT779.G75 2011
  746.44'5--dc23
                      2011019345

COVER AND TITLE PAGE: BALL JOINTS, detail.
Full quilt on page 74.

DEDICATIONS

FROM DAPHNE

This book is dedicated to my dearest friend, Moira Cannata. Moira's enthusiasm and passion for quilting and many forms of needlework was inspiring to all who knew her. Moira was my greatest cheerleader and I will miss her very much.

FROM SUSAN

We are blessed with a rich legacy of friends, mentors, and sister quilters who have enriched our lives with their knowledge and experience, but most importantly, with their love. We are humbled and thankful to have these "sisters in cloth" touch us so deeply.

THIS PAGE AND OPPOSITE: FRENCH COUNTRY *DANSE*, detail. Full quilt on page 24.

ACKNOWLEDGMENTS

We have many people to thank who support us, both professionally and personally. First, the members of our quilt groups, the Loose Threads Sewciety and the Spoolboard Quilters. We thank you for your friendship.

Second, thanks also to:

The Warm Company, makers of Lite Steam-a-Seam 2®, the "secret ingredient" for our Give and Take Appliqué™ technique.

Patti Carey, Director of Marketing for Northcottt/Lyndhurst. Your support of our company is greatly appreciated.

Lissa Alexander, Director of Marketing, Moda Fabrics, for the French reproduction fabrics for FRENCH COUNTRY *DANSE*.

Sue Penn, owner and designer, Fine Lines Fabric, for Bistro fabrics for the NEW YORK BEAUTY TABLE RUNNER.

Bob and Heather Purcell, Superior Threads. Your threads truly ARE superior.

Arlene MacKenzie, On Point Quilting Studio, and Phyllis Wright, Quilting Sew Fine, for longarm quilting services.

Thank you to the professional staff at the American Quilter's Society, who turn our designs and words into outstanding books that inspire quilters. We would especially like to acknowledge Andi Reynolds, executive book editor; Linda Lasco, editor of this book; Melissa Potterbaum, our book's designer; and Charles R. Lynch, photographer.

And finally, thanks to our families for all their support and encouragement. Special thanks from Daphne to her husband, Alan, and from Susan to her husband, Henry.

Special thanks to Higdon Furniture in Paducah, Kentucky, for photo settings.

THIS PAGE AND OPPOSITE: SUPER NOVA, detail.
Full quilt on page 32.

TABLE OF CONTENTS

INTRODUCTION

We are very excited about Give and Take Appliqué™ and know you will have fun with the designs in this book. There is an infinite range of possibilities with our "two for one" technique: design and layout options, quilt size and color choices, and a wide range of stitch opportunities.

We have been working with this design concept since 2006 and have published a series of patterns and several magazine articles about using the technique. This book is the result of thinking about traditional quilt patterns, commonly constructed with traditional methods, and wondering how we could make these designs using Give and Take Appliqué. We found we could make designs like New York Beauty, Double Wedding Ring, Pickle Dish, Orange Peel, Robbing Peter to Pay Paul, and Drunkard's Path easier and more enjoyable. Several of the projects have a contemporary look due to the fabrics and colors we selected for our quilts.

We invite you to come along with us on this journey into the world of Give and Take Appliqué. Here is the best way for you to get the most from this book:

Take a few minutes and read Chapter 1, Fabric Fundamentals. You will find many useful tips on color choices, pattern print size, and the importance of value when making your quilts.

Chapter 2, Tools and Technique, describes the tools you will need and how to choose the best fusible web. Included is an in-depth look at the wide variety of stitch options for your appliqué. There is lots of fun at the sewing machine using decorative stitches for machine appliqué. This chapter also shows you the detailed technique steps for Give and Take Appliqué.

Next, work through Chapter 3, the first project, NEW YORK BEAUTY TABLE RUNNER. It is an excellent introduction to the technique and will help you understand the correct sequence of steps to trace, fuse, cut, and sew.

After you have made your table runner, you will have a thorough understanding of Give and Take Appliqué and you will be ready to make any of the other projects in the book.

Please send us photographs so we can see how you interpret our designs. See Resources (page 78) for our contact information.

THIS PAGE: COSMO CURVES, detail. Full quilt on page 50.

We most commonly use cotton fabrics for our quilts. We choose the best quality fabrics for superior results. Sometimes we can't find the exact fabric we want so we will consider other fabric types. For *Grandma's Pawpaws* (page 60), Daphne chose a striped silk fabric for the inner border and backed it with a lightweight fusible interfacing to stabilize the fabric and prevent fraying. You may want to consider other fabric options. We recommend you test the fabric first to ensure it will work well in your project. For example: cut and sew a sample and then wash it if you intend your project to be washable.

The most important factors when selecting fabrics for Give and Take Appliqué are value and scale. Contrast between the background and the appliqué shapes will result in the most successful projects.

What Is Value?

Value refers to the relative lightness or darkness of fabric. The key item in this statement is the word "relative." This means that you need to compare one fabric to another to see if one is lighter in value or darker in value. Looking at a fabric by itself cannot tell you its value. When you compare that fabric with another one, you can say it is lighter or darker. Here are pictures of pairs of fabrics. Which one is lighter than the other one?

Two blue fabrics

Blue and turquoise fabrics

It is easy to answer the question for the first pair of fabrics. The fabric on the left is lighter than the one on the right. In the other pair, it is a little trickier. The different colors of the fabrics make it more difficult to decide. What if the color wasn't there? Would it be easier or more difficult to determine relative value?

Grayscale fabrics

Here is the same picture converted to grayscale—only shades of gray are used in the picture.

This time it's easier to see that the fabric on the left is the darker one.

Value plays a very important role in Give and Take Appliqué. If there is low-value contrast (that is, the values are very close) the design will not be visible. We suggest that you choose fabrics where it is very easy to determine which fabric is lighter and which fabric is darker. Subtle value differences will not be as effective.

How Does Fabric Scale Influence Choices?

Another important consideration is the fabric scale. Scale refers to the size of the design. Small-scale fabrics are generally prints that duplicate the design elements in a regular pattern. Large-scale fabrics commonly have large areas of a background color or large motifs that are predominately one color. If you use large-scale fabrics in these designs, the appliqué shapes may include both light and dark values. This can obscure the design details.

Large-scale multicolor fabric

Poor (left) and good (right) background choices for the large-scale fabric

Background and Appliqué—Choosing the Values

If a light-value fabric is appliquéd on a dark print there can be shadowing—the dark print can show through the light appliqué fabric. To prevent this, in Give and Take Appliqué the appliqué shapes are **always** the darker-value fabrics. Remember this rule when you select fabrics for the projects.

Directional Fabrics

Some of the projects in our book use directional fabrics in different ways. A little extra planning will help you be successful with your Give and Take Appliqué quilt. For example, the outer blocks in HOT TAMALES (page 54) are made from a striped fabric that is strip-cut and then sub-cut into triangles. As a result the outer blocks have bias edges. Susan took extra care when sewing them together so they did not stretch.

Daphne cut the outer border strips for GRANDMA'S PAWPAWS (page 60) lengthwise to take advantage of the strong vertical design in the fabric. The strips were centered on the same repeating motif for each of the four border strips.

Color Choices

Color is probably the most personal decision when we choose fabric for a quilt. We can be motivated by a variety of emotions, thoughts, habits, or trends. We feel that if you work with colors you like, you will enjoy making your project. You may want to think about where you will use the quilt. Should it match the décor of your bedroom or living room and enhance the furnishings and wall color?

If your quilt is a gift, does the recipient like a combination of blues and purples? Perhaps your favorite fabric company has designed a lovely collection with an exciting border print that you can't turn down. Most often we have already narrowed down the options when we visit the quilt store or open the drawers in our sewing room.

If you are concerned about making color choices for your quilts, let our quilts guide you. At the beginning of each project chapter, we have described our choices and made suggestions for alternate color combinations. Check fabric company websites to see what they offer and, most importantly, visit your local quilt shop and have their experienced staff offer ideas and tips for choosing fabrics.

All the Give and Take Appliqué designs are suitable for a wide range of color choices and there are no wrong color decisions. We want the quilts to appeal to a broad range of tastes and we hope you will be able to envision your Give and Take Appliqué in the color combinations and schemes that appeal to you.

TOOLS AND TECHNIQUES

Tools

Using good quality tools will make quilting a more pleasurable experience. You probably have most of the equipment you need for the projects in the book. Visit your local quilt shop or shop online for any of the items you are missing.

Tracing Tools

Use a pencil, mechanical pencil, or fine point permanent marker and a drafting ruler to trace the pattern.

You will trace the appliqué patterns onto the release paper of fusible web. For this step you will need a sharp pencil and, in some cases, a ruler. We like mechanical pencils for tracing the pattern.

You may want to use a fine point permanent marker like Sharpie®. Test your marker to be sure it dries quickly without smudging. For tracing straight lines we like to use a clear plastic or drafting ruler (minimum length of 18"). Look for this at an art or office supply store. We find these rulers easier to use than our rotary-cutting rulers since they are thinner and we can see the edge to trace accurately.

Template Plastic

Many of the designs require tracing the pattern several times. We make this step faster and more accurate by making plastic templates for the appliqué pattern. We prefer template plastic without gridlines.

Use plastic templates to trace the shapes onto fusible web.

To create tracing templates:

1. Cut a piece of template plastic the same size as the block pattern. Refer to the individual project instructions for the size to cut.
2. Trace the block pattern onto the plastic with a pencil and mark each section with the block name and size.
3. Cut the plastic apart **continuously** on the traced lines, being careful to cut smooth curves and sharp points. Use a pair of small sharp scissors for this step.
4. Use the shapes to trace the pattern onto the fusible web.

Cutting Tools

Rotary Cutter, Ruler, and Mat

You will need these tools to cut your fabric into squares or rectangles as required by the project. Change the blade when the cutter becomes dull to ensure accurate cuts and close your cutter and store it carefully when it is not being used. A variety of ruler sizes will make cutting easier. We particularly recommend 12½" or 15" square rulers to square up your blocks.

Scissors

We recommend several pairs of scissors for cutting the fused fabric into shapes. Look for scissors that are sharp right out to the point, not with a blunt tip. We use medium-sized scissors that feel comfortable in our hand. We also use smaller sharp-to-the-point scissors for cutting smaller pieces.

Clean and sharpen your scissors regularly; remove any sticky residue that builds up from the fusible web. We use a small amount of nail polish remover on a cotton pad to clean the blades.

Another option for cutting the fused fabric is an art knife. Be sure to replace the blade when it becomes dull for best results.

Sewing Machine

Our usual stitch of choice for appliqué is a zigzag stitch. Your sewing machine should have a zigzag stitch adjustable both in width and length. We also like to use the decorative stitches on our sewing machine. Different machines will have different built-in stitches. We will discuss options later in this chapter.

It is helpful to use an open-toe foot so you can clearly see where you are stitching. If this is not included in the range of sewing machine feet that came with your machine, contact your local dealer to see if one is available.

Use an open-toe foot to clearly see where to stitch.

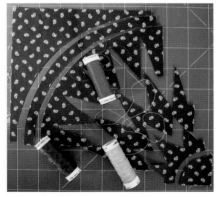

Choose thread to match or contrast with the appliqué shapes.

Thread

The stitching line that holds the appliqué fabric in place is functional; it secures the fused shape onto the background. It can also be a design element. Your choice will influence the thread you use for the appliqué. Options include a fine thread that matches the appliqué shapes, medium-weight thread that contrasts with the appliqué shape, and heavy thread used to stitch a decorative design around or on the appliqué shapes.

Tools and Techniques

You will also need thread for piecing blocks together. We use 50-wt 100 percent cotton thread for piecing. Choose a thread that will blend with your fabrics. Our favorites are neutral colors like cream, gray, beige, or tan.

For quilting we use a wide range of threads. Invisible polyester thread is useful for stitching around appliqué shapes. Variegated cotton, rayon, or polyester threads are available in a

A variety of decorative threads can be used for quilting.

wide range of colors to coordinate with any fabrics. Be sure to use the needle size recommended for your thread choice.

Machine Needles

For piecing, we recommend a Universal or Jeans/Denim 80/12 needle. Embroidery needles (75/11) are useful for machine appliqué with fine threads. Metafil or metallic needles work best with rayon and delicate threads. Topstitch (90/14) needles are useful for machine quilting with heavier threads. Check with your machine dealer for the brand they recommend for your sewing machine and also see if the thread manufacturer recommends a needle size for their thread. We begin each new project with a fresh needle and make sure the needle is properly inserted into the machine before we begin stitching.

Sometimes your machine needle will pick up sticky residue from the fusible web when stitching down the appliqué shapes. We use a small piece of batting

to wipe the needle; others prefer to use a little nail polish remover. Remember to check your needle for burrs or rough spots and replace the needle if you find any. It is also important to change your needle frequently. Piercing fused fabric with an old needle can damage the fabric or leave large holes.

Fusible Web

Fusible web is the key ingredient in Give and Take Appliqué. We use the web to bond or "glue" the appliqué shapes to the background fabrics. Fusible web is a man-made fiber that will melt when heated. When placed between two pieces of fabric, the melting action of the web causes it to fuse the fabrics together. The fused fabric is stable, easy to cut, and resists distortion at the bias edges.

Fusible web comes in a range of types, almost all of them attached to a release paper on one or both sides, which stays attached until you remove it after the ironing process.

We prefer a lightweight web that has release paper on both sides. This means the web will not stick to the pattern when you trace it and ensures the fusible does not separate from the release paper until you want it to. Be sure you use a fusible web that can be sewn and if you are planning on making a project that will be washed, make certain that the fusible web can be washed as well. If you are unsure whether you can sew and wash your projects, we recommend testing them before using them in your projects.

Fusible web comes in a range of sizes; generally you can buy 12", 18", or 24" widths cut from a roll. All fusible web requirements in the materials lists for the projects are based on the 12" width.

Keep your fusible web rolled rather than folded so it will not separate from the release paper. Large pieces can be rolled on an empty tube or bolt insert. Your local quilt shop may have a bolt insert that they would be happy to give you.

Some fusible web is sold with a plastic instruction sheet wrapped around it. Keep this with your fusible to remind you of the brand and type since fusing instructions may vary for different products. Some fusible web will deteriorate with age, so don't use web that is several years old and do keep the web away from direct sunlight.

Remember that longer isn't necessarily better. Read and follow the manufacturers directions for fusing time. Different products will vary in the amount of time needed for a good bond. Leaving the iron on longer can damage the fabrics and may make the appliqué fall off. Make some test swatches and keep notes on the settings for your iron and the optimal time for fusing.

Appliqué Pressing Sheets

We cannot stress enough how important it is to use a Teflon® appliqué pressing sheet when working with fusible web to protect both the ironing board and your iron. Many quilting disasters have happened when the iron meets the fusible web without the protection of a pressing sheet! Always use the sheet, even when it's just a quick little touch up. There are many different pressing sheets available; your quilt shop staff will be able to offer suggestions of the best brands. If your budget allows, buy two sheets and sandwich your appliqué between them. This will protect both your ironing surface and your iron.

To clean your pressing sheet, wipe with a scrap of cotton batting on both sides or use a damp cloth. Leave the sheet open to dry. Most sheets can be folded or rolled for storage.

Techniques

The basic steps for all Give and Take Appliqué designs are the same. Read this section and refer to it when you make any of the projects in the book. We recommend you make the first project, New York Beauty Table Runner (page 20), before you work on the other designs. By doing this you will have the confidence to make good fabric choices and understand the method completely.

Making the Blocks

1. Cut fusible web squares or rectangles required for the project using rotary-cutting tools. Also cut the light and dark fabrics listed in the cutting directions.

Fusible web and fabrics for 2 blocks

Trace the appliqué pattern on precut fusible web.

2. Prepare the appliqué shapes by positioning the precut fusible web over the appliqué pattern (paper-side up). Trace the design onto the paper side of the web with a sharp pencil.

Helpful Hints for Tracing:

Option 1
Position the precut fusible web over the appliqué pattern and trace on the paper side of fusible web.

Option 2
Make plastic templates (page 10) for the block and use them for tracing.

Option 3
Make templates from freezer paper and use them for tracing.

Cut 4 freezer paper squares (or rectangles) the same size as the appliqué pattern.

Trace the appliqué pattern on the paper side of one piece of freezer paper and mark each part with the block name and size.

With a dry iron, iron the shiny side of one piece of freezer paper to the paper side of a second freezer paper square. Repeat until all four pieces are ironed together, with the traced pattern on top.

Cut the stack apart on the traced lines continuously, being careful to cut smooth curves and sharp points.

Trace the shapes onto the fusible web.

Make tracing templates using stacked freezer paper.

Fuse the web to the wrong side of the dark fabric.

3.   Following the manufacturer's directions and using an appliqué pressing sheet, fuse the traced fusible web onto the wrong side of the dark fabric squares (or rectangles), paper-side up and fusible-side down. Make sure all areas are pressed well.

Cut the fused fabric into shapes.

4.   Let the fused fabric cool. Use a sharp pair of scissors to cut the fused fabric apart **continuously** on the traced lines.

5.   To fuse the appliqué shapes to the background, remove the release paper from the back of one set of shapes and arrange them alternately on two backgrounds.

Match the outer straight edges of the shapes with the edges of the background fabric. To assist with placement, use your templates as a guide. If you did not use templates, use the release paper removed from one piece to help position the next piece.

When you are pleased with the arrangement, cover the blocks with an appliqué pressing sheet and fuse the shapes to the background.

Arrange and fuse the shapes onto two background squares.

6.   There are several ways to appliqué the edges of the shapes. Most of the time we use a narrow zigzag stitch using thread to match the appliqué. Our preferred thread for this method is a 60-wt fine thread. We always position the appliqué shape to the left of the needle when stitching.

Appliqué Stitching Techniques

For zigzag stitching, thread your machine with thread to match the appliqué shapes both on the top and in the bobbin. Set your machine to a narrow zigzag and stitch over the raw edges of the shapes. The stitch should be completely on the appliqué shape, with the needle just piercing the background when it stitches to the right. Use an open-toe embroidery foot for best visibility. You do not need to stitch on the outside edges of the blocks.

To ensure smooth curves, you need to stop and pivot the work as you sew. The tighter the curve, the more frequently you will need to pivot. It is important that the needle remains in the fabric when you lift the presser foot to turn the work. Use the needle-down option if your machine has one. It is also important that the needle is in the correct position when you turn your work. To stitch an appliqué shape with an outside (convex) curve, pivot when the needle is on the background fabric. To stitch inside (concave) curves, pivot when the needle is on the appliqué shape itself.

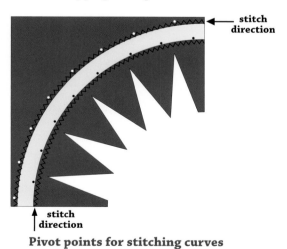

Pivot points for stitching curves

Some of our designs include deep V shapes and sharp points. The close-up photograph below show

how we stitch these areas. We used contrasting thread for better visibility for the photograph.

Deep V shapes and sharp points appliquéd with a zigzag stitch. (Contrasting thread color used for visibility.)

If your stitching puckers the block, try lowering the top tension slightly. If you still have puckers, pin a stabilizer to the back of the blocks and remove it after the stitching is complete.

Decorative Stitching Options

Many of us have sewing machines with lots of built-in decorative stitches. Do you use them? They are often a selling feature when we buy our machines but we do not think of using them with our normal sewing and quilting. Many of the stitches are very effective as appliqué stitches.

Your machine has small drawings of each of the built-in decorative stitches, either on the machine itself, or on a separate plastic card. We think of these as an artist's renditions. When the stitches are sewn they may appear a bit different from the diagrams. For this reason we recommend you sew every decorative stitch so you will know exactly what it looks like. Use a wide foot since the needle moves from side to side for most stitches.

Daphne's machine has 180 built-in stitches! It takes some time to try them all, and to change the width and length of each one to see more variations. This can be a rather boring task to do at one sitting. We suggest you spend a few minutes before each sewing session to stitch 2 or 3 of the stitches. Use a piece of muslin and place a stabilizer on the back. This is especially helpful if the stitch is a wide one; it will help prevent puckering. Write the stitch number and the width and length beside the row of stitching. If you change these, be sure to make note of those settings as well. Keep using the same piece of muslin so all your stitches will be in one place. This will be an excellent reference for future projects where decorative stitches can be used.

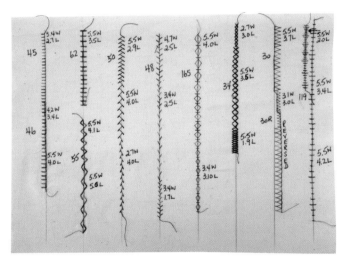

Stitch-outs of decorative machine stitches

If you want to use one of your decorative stitches for appliqué you need to be familiar with the pattern of stitching. By this we mean, does the needle stitch one stitch forward and then one to the left and then one to the right? Or does it stitch forward, right and then left? You need to know exactly where the needle will stitch so you can anticipate pivot points for curves and corners. Before trying a decorative stitch on your project, set up a small sample and test the stitching. This gives you the opportunity to understand exactly how the stitch is made, and you can make

adjustments in width, length, and tension. Another consideration is the color and type of thread to use with these stitches. Select a contrasting color so the stitching is visible. Variegated threads work well on some stitches but not those that go backwards and then forward. Thick threads can build up too much with some stitches. Test the stitch and the thread before working on your project.

Some examples of decorative machine stitching for appliqué are shown in the pictures below.

NEW YORK BEAUTY TABLE RUNNER with decorative machine stitching

Some decorative stitches that do not work well for appliqué can add a unique touch to your quilts. Daphne used a variety of stitches on top of the fused appliqué shapes for her CHUTES & LADDERS quilt (page 29). She tested many stitches on fused fabric samples before selecting the stitches for her project.

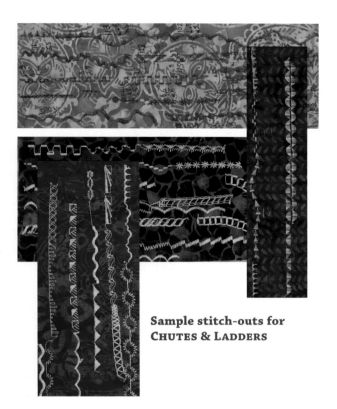

**Sample stitch-outs for
CHUTES & LADDERS**

Finishing

Follow these general instructions for
borders and binding unless specific
border steps are included in the project
chapter.

Borders

Cut border strips the width specified
in the pattern; join them as necessary.

Measure the length of the quilt and cut
two borders to that measurement.

Sew to the sides of the quilt top and press
the seams toward the border.

Measure the width of the quilt including the two
side borders and cut two borders to match. Sew
to the top and bottom of the quilt top and press
as before.

Binding

Sew the 2¼" strips together with 45-degree
diagonal seams and press the seams open.

Fold the binding in half lengthwise and press
to make a double-fold binding.

Sew the binding to the front of the quilted quilt,
forming a miter at each corner.

Trim the batting and backing, then turn the
binding to the back and slipstitch the folded edge
in place by hand.

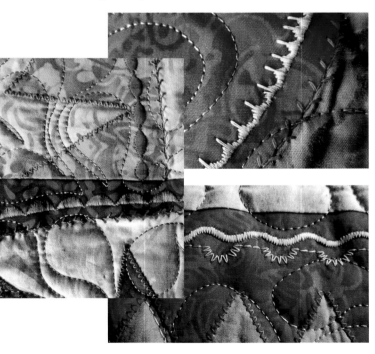

**CHUTES & LADDERS with decorative
machine stitching on the appliqué shapes**

CHAPTER 3
NEW YORK BEAUTY PROJECTS

There are two projects in this chapter, both based on a New York Beauty block. We suggest you make the table runner first, before any other project in the book. It is a small project, everyone can use a new table runner, and it is the best way to learn our Give and Take Appliqué technique. You need basic quilting skills to make the runner.

New York Beauty Table Runner, detail.
Full quilt on page 20.

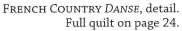

Daphne made her table runner using fabrics to match her everyday dishes. This design is suitable for Christmas fabrics or other seasonal prints. Choose fabrics that have high-value contrast and ones that are small scale for best results. Be sure to read Fabric Fundamentals (page 7) for more information about fabric selection.

The bed quilt uses the same block design in a different size. A coordinating set of French reproduction fabrics gives the quilt a classic, fresh look. The quilt would be equally effective as a scrap quilt, as long as attention is paid to strong value contrast.

French Country *Danse*, detail.
Full quilt on page 24.

New York Beauty Table Runner

NEW YORK BEAUTY TABLE RUNNER, 16½" x 42½", made by Daphne Greig

Finished block size: 6" x 6"; Number of blocks: 12

Materials

* Block background—light print, ½ yard
* Block appliqué—dark print, ⅓ yard
* Sashing and binding—very dark print, ½ yard
* Border—medium print, ¼ yard
* Backing, ¾ yard
* Batting, 20" x 46"
* Fusible Web, 1¼ yards

Cutting Instructions

Cut all strips across the width of fabric.

Block background (light print)
* 2 strips 6½" wide, cut into 12 squares 6½" x 6½"

Block appliqué (dark print)
* 1 strip 6½" wide, cut into 6 squares 6½" x 6½"

Sashing and binding
* 6 strips 1" wide
  From 2 strips cut 10 rectangles 1" x 6½" for sashing. The remaining 4 strips will be trimmed to fit after the rows of blocks are joined together.

* 4 strips 2¼" wide; set aside for binding

Border
* 3 strips 2" wide
  These will be trimmed to fit after the center of the runner is sewn.

Fusible Web
* 6 squares 6½" x 6½"

Making the Blocks

Step 1: Prepare the appliqué shapes:

Step 1: Trace the design onto fusible web squares.

Position a square of fusible web over the pattern (paper side facing you) and trace the design with a sharp pencil. Repeat with the remaining squares for a total of 6 traced squares. See page 14 for hints to make tracing easier.

Step 2: Fabric preparation and fusing:
Following the manufacturer's directions and using an appliqué pressing sheet, fuse the traced squares onto the wrong side of the 6 dark print squares, paper-side up and fusible-side down. Make sure all areas are pressed well.

Step 2: Fuse the traced squares to the wrong side of the dark fabric squares.

Step 3: Cutting the appliqué shapes:
Let the fused fabric cool. Use a sharp pair of scissors to cut **continuously** on the traced lines. You will get 6 shapes from each fused dark square.

Step 3: Cut the fused fabric to make 6 shapes from each square.

Step 4: Fusing the appliqué shapes to the background squares:
Remove the paper from the back of one set of shapes and arrange them alternately on two background squares. (See photo, page 22).

Match the outer straight edges of the shapes with the edges of the background squares, using the templates or the paper removed from the shapes to help with positioning.

When you are pleased with the placement, cover the blocks with an appliqué pressing sheet and fuse the shapes to the background blocks. Make a total of 12 blocks.

Step 4: Arrange and fuse the shapes alternately on two background squares.

Step 5: Stitching around the shapes:
Use zigzag or a decorative stitch to sew the raw edges of the appliqué shapes. (See page 15 for details about stitching techniques and options.)

Making the Runner

Arrange the blocks and the 1" x 6½" sashing rectangles in two rows, referring to the runner picture and the assembly diagram. Sew the rows together with ¼" seams and press the seam allowances toward the sashing.

Measure the block rows and cut 3 strips from the remaining 1" sashing strips to match the measurement. Sew one strip between the rows and one to each side. Press seam allowances toward the sashing.

Measure the width of the runner and cut 2 sashing strips to match. Sew to the ends of the runner.

Add the outer border. Measure the length of the runner and cut 2 borders to match. Sew to the sides of the runner and press toward the border. Measure the width of the runner and cut 2 borders to match. Sew these strips to the ends and press toward the border.

Quilting:
Sandwich the quilt top, batting, and backing and baste well. Daphne quilted in the ditch around each block and around each fused shape, close to the appliqué stitching.

Binding:
Sew the 2¼" strips together with 45-degree diagonal seams and press the seams open. Fold the binding in half to make a double fold binding and sew it all around the edge. Turn the binding to the back and slipstitch the folded edge in place by hand.

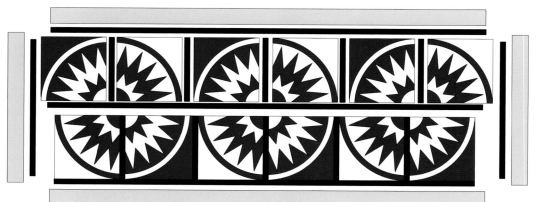

Quilt assembly

Template for NEW YORK BEAUTY TABLE RUNNER—6½" unfinished block

French Country *Danse*

FRENCH COUNTRY *DANSE*, 75½" x 89½", made by Daphne Greig, quilted by Arlene MacKenzie

Finished block size: 7" x 7"; Number of blocks: 80

Materials

* Block background—4 light prints,
  1 yard EACH (4 yards total)
* Block appliqué—8 dark prints,
  ¼ yard EACH (2 yards total)

* First border and binding, 1¼ yards
* Second border, ½ yard
* Outer border (cut lengthwise), 2¼ yards
* Backing, 5½ yards
* Batting, 83" x 97"
* Fusible web, 8½ yards

Cutting Instructions

Cut all strips across the width of fabric unless otherwise noted.

Light prints
* 4 strips 7½" wide from EACH fabric,
  cut into 20 squares (total of 80 squares)

Dark prints
* 1 strip 7½" wide from EACH fabric,
  cut into 5 squares (total 40 squares)

First border and binding
* 16 strips 2¼" wide

Second border
* 7 strips 1½" wide

Outer border (cut lengthwise)
* 4 strips 7½" wide

Fusible web
* 40 squares 7½" x 7½"

Making the Blocks

Step 1: Prepare the appliqué shapes, tracing the design with a sharp pencil onto the fusible web. Make 40 traced squares.

Step 1

Step 2: Fuse the traced squares onto the wrong side of the dark print squares.

Step 2

Step 3: Use a sharp pair of scissors to cut **continuously** on the traced line. You will have 6 shapes cut from each fused dark square.

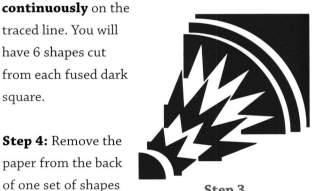

Step 3

Step 4: Remove the paper from the back of one set of shapes and arrange them alternately on 2 matching background squares. When you are pleased with the placement, cover the blocks with an appliqué pressing sheet and fuse the shapes to the background blocks. Make a total of 80 blocks.

Step 4

Step 5: Use zigzag or a decorative stitch to sew the raw edges of the appliqué shapes.

Making the Quilt

Referring to the quilt assembly diagram below, arrange the blocks in 10 rows of 8 blocks each. A design wall is helpful for this step to distribute the colors evenly throughout the quilt. Sew the blocks together in rows, then sew the rows together. Press the seams open for a flatter quilt.

Adding the Borders

Add the first border using the 2¼" wide strips.

Add the second border using the 1½" strips.

Add the third border using the 7½" strips.

Sandwich the quilt top, batting, and backing, and baste well. Our friend Arlene quilted an allover design adapted from the designs in the border fabric.

Trim and bind the quilt.

Quilt assembly

Template for FRENCH COUNTRY *DANSE*—7½" unfinished block

Enlarge pattern 125%

CHAPTER 4
RECTANGLE BEAUTY PROJECTS

The projects in this chapter originated with asking, "What if?" What if the New York Beauty block was made as a rectangle instead of a square? The result is Rectangle Beauty, an intriguing asymmetrical block with many possibilities.

CHUTES & LADDERS, detail.
Full quilt on page 29.

For easy placement and piecing, the blocks needed additional rectangles to make them square. A second block, Spike Rectangle, was designed. CHUTES & LADDERS uses bright batik fabrics with strong contrast. Fabrics were chosen to coordinate with the border fabric, and rows of Spike Rectangle blocks are used as an inner border around the quilt. There are several possible arrangements so we recommend you work with a design wall when arranging the blocks for your quilt.

SUPER NOVA was the result of a happy accident when Daphne reversed the tracing templates for one set of blocks. The resulting mirror image created the circular design. (This reinforces the importance of labelling tracing templates!) The fabrics in this quilt are modern and fresh. Again, good value contrast is important for this design.

SUPER NOVA, detail.
Full quilt on page 32.

Chutes & Ladders

CHUTES & LADDERS, 50" x 50", made by Daphne Greig

Finished blocks: 16 Rectangle Beauty blocks: 6" x 9",
32 Spike Rectangle blocks: 3" x 9"

Materials

✳ Block background—4 light prints
   ½ yard EACH (2 yards total)

✳ Block appliqué—4 dark prints,
   ½ yard EACH (2 yards total)

✳ Border & binding, 1 yard

✳ Backing, 3½ yards

✳ Batting, 58" x 58"

✳ Fusible Web, 3 yards

Cutting Instructions

Cut all strips across the width of fabric.

Block background (4 light prints)
✳ 4 rectangles 6½" x 9½" from EACH fabric
(total 16 rectangles)
✳ 8 rectangles 3½" x 9½" from EACH fabric
(total of 32 rectangles)

Block appliqué (4 dark prints)
✳ 2 rectangles 6½" x 9½" from EACH fabric
(total of 8 rectangles)

✳ 4 rectangles 3½" x 9½" from EACH fabric
(total of 16 rectangles)
✳ Select 2 of the fabrics and cut 2 squares
3½" x 3½" from EACH for spike border
cornerstones.

Border and Binding
✳ 5 strips 4½" wide
✳ 5 strips 2¼" wide

Fusible Web
✳ 8 rectangles 6½" x 9½"
✳ 16 rectangles 3½" x 9½"

Making the Blocks

Step 1: Trace 8 Rectangle Beauty patterns (page 35) onto 6½" x 9½" rectangles of fusible web. Trace 16 Spike Rectangle patterns (page 36) onto 3½" x 9½" rectangles of fusible web.

Step 1

Step 2: Fuse the traced rectangles to the wrong side of the dark fabric rectangles. Use a sharp pair of scissors to cut **continuously** on the traced lines.

Cut each Rectangle Beauty fused fabric into 5 shapes.

Cut each Spike Rectangle fused fabric into 2 shapes.

Step 2

Step 3: Arrange each set of shapes alternately on two matching background rectangles and fuse in place. Make a total of 16 Rectangle Beauty blocks and 32 Spike Rectangle blocks.

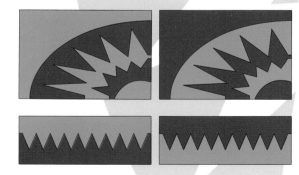

Step 3

Step 4: Use a zigzag or decorative stitch to sew the raw edges of the appliqué shapes. Daphne added decorative stitches on the appliqué shapes of her quilt.

Quilt assembly

Making the Quilt

Arrange the 16 Rectangle Beauty blocks and 16 of the Spike Rectangle blocks in rows, referring to the quilt photograph (page 29) and the assembly diagram or trying other arrangements on your design wall. When you are happy with the design, sew the Spike Rectangles to the Rectangle Beauty blocks to make squares. Then sew the squares together in rows and sew the rows together. Press the seams open.

Make 4 Spike Rectangle borders, each with 4 of the remaining blocks. Sew 2 borders to the sides of the quilt. Add the 3½" cornerstones to the ends of the remaining 2 borders and add to the top and bottom.

Add the outer border using the 4½" wide strips.

Sandwich the quilt top, batting, and backing, and baste well. Daphne quilted a swirling design over the center of the quilt with variegated polyester thread in colors to coordinate with the fabrics. For the border she quilted a loose petal design.

Trim and bind the quilt.

Super Nova

SUPER NOVA, 40" x 43", made by Daphne Greig

Finished blocks: 8 Rectangle Beauty blocks and 8 blocks reversed: 6" x 9",
12 Spike Rectangle blocks: 3" x 9"

Materials
* Rectangle Beauty background—2 light prints, ½ yard EACH
* Rectangle Beauty appliqué—2 dark prints, ¼ yard EACH
* Spike Rectangle background—2 medium/light prints, ¼ yard EACH
* Spike Rectangle appliqué—2 medium prints, ¼ yard EACH
* Border & binding, ½ yard
* Backing, 3 yards
* Batting, 48" x 51"
* Fusible web, 2¼ yards

Cutting Instructions
Cut all strips across the width of fabric.

Rectangle Beauty background (2 light prints)
* 8 rectangles 6½" x 9½" from EACH fabric (total 16 rectangles)

Rectangle Beauty appliqué (2 dark prints)
* 4 rectangles 6½" x 9½" from EACH fabric (total of 8 rectangles)

Spike Rectangle background (2 medium/light prints)
* 6 rectangles 3½" x 9½" from EACH fabric (total 12 rectangles)

Spike Rectangle appliqué (2 medium prints)
* 3 rectangles 3½" x 9½" from EACH fabric (total 6 rectangles)

Border
* 4 strips 4" wide

Binding
* 5 strips 2¼" wide

Fusible Web
* 8 rectangles 6½" x 9½"
* 6 rectangles 3½" x 9½"

Making the Rectangle Beauty Blocks

Step 1: Make a template of the Rectangle Beauty block pattern (page 35).

Trace 4 Rectangle Beauty and 4 **reversed** Rectangle Beauty patterns onto 6½" x 9½" fusible web rectangles.

Step 1

Step 2: Fuse the traced Rectangle Beauty and **reversed** Rectangle Beauty rectangles to the wrong side of the dark fabric rectangles—2 each on the 2 different appliqué fabrics.

Cut the fused fabric into 5 shapes each, cutting **continuously** on the traced lines. Keep the shapes for the blocks and reversed blocks in separate piles.

Step 2

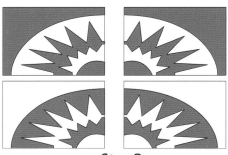

Step 3

Step 3: Remove the paper from the backs and arrange the Rectangle Beauty shapes alternately on 8 background rectangles, 4 of each fabric. Fuse in place. Repeat with the reversed shapes.

Step 4: Use a zigzag or decorative stitch to sew the raw edges of the appliqué shapes.

Making the Spike Rectangle Blocks

Step 1: Trace the Spike Rectangle pattern (page 36) onto the six 3½" x 9½" fusible web rectangles.

Step 1

Step 2: Fuse the traced rectangles to the wrong side of the medium fabric rectangles. Cut the fused fabric into 2 shapes each, cutting **continuously** on the traced lines.

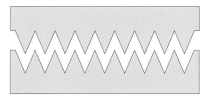

Step 2

Step 3: Arrange sets of Spike Rectangle shapes on the background rectangles for 12 blocks, 6 of each fabric combination. Fuse in place.

Step 3

Step 4: Use a zigzag or decorative stitch to sew the raw edges of the appliqué shapes.

Making the Quilt

Arrange and sew the Rectangle Beauty, **reversed** Rectangle Beauty, and Spike Rectangle blocks as shown. Press the seams open.

Add the outer border using the 4" wide strips.

Sandwich the quilt top, batting, and backing, and baste well. Daphne quilted a wave and spiral design on the light and medium/light areas of the quilt using variegated polyester thread. In the border she quilted a continuous spiral design.

Trim and bind the quilt.

Quilt assembly

**Rectangle Beauty template for Chutes & Ladders
and Super Nova—6½" x 9½"**

Enlarge pattern 125%

**Spike Rectangle template for
Chutes & Ladders and
Super Nova—3½" x 9½"**

CHAPTER 5
WEDDING RING PROJECTS

WEDDING RING QUILTS ARE ALWAYS A FAVORITE TO COMMEMORATE SPECIAL EVENTS SUCH AS A MARRIAGE OR ANNIVERSARY. WITH THE GIVE AND TAKE APPLIQUÉ TECHNIQUE, BLOCK CONSTRUCTION HAS NEVER BEEN EASIER! THE ARCS ARE SIMPLE TO CUT AND APPLIQUÉ IN PLACE AND THE STITCHING CAN INCLUDE A VARIETY OF STYLES AND COLORS. THE CORNER TRIANGLES ADD COLOR TO THE SIMPLE DESIGN AND ADDITIONAL BORDERS CAN INCLUDE FLORAL APPLIQUÉ FOR A ROMANTIC TOUCH.

LUPINE RINGS, detail.
Full quilt on page 38.

Scrappy blocks are a popular choice for this design and LUPINE RINGS features complementary colors of purple and yellow to great advantage. Susan chose a range from orange to soft yellow and from deep violet to strong blue/purple. This design would work with commemorative photos, printed on fabric, in the centers of the blocks with dark rings.

I DO! I DO! showcases a black-and-white fabric collection that provides a strong contrast but that is softened by the rich pinks and lush greens in the appliqué. Other color choices could be guided by newlyweds' favorites.

I DO! I DO!, detail.
Full quilt on page 42.

Lupine Rings

LUPINE RINGS, 38" x 58", made by Susan Purney Mark, quilted by Arlene Mackenzie

Finished block size: 10" x 10"; Number of blocks: 15

Materials

* Block and border background—a variety of light prints to total 3 yards
* Block and border appliqué—a variety of dark prints to total 1⅞ yards

* Binding, ½ yard
* Backing (pieced crosswise), 2¾ yards
* Batting, 46" x 66"
* Fusible Web, 4 yards

Cutting Instructions

Cut all strips across the width of fabric.

Block background (light prints)
* 5 strips 10½" wide, cut into 15 squares 10½" x 10½"
* 6 strips 4½" wide, cut into 16 rectangles 4½" x 10½"
* 3 strips 2⅜" wide, cut into 48 squares 2⅜" x 2⅜"

Block appliqué (dark prints)
* 3 strips 10½" wide, cut into 8 squares 10½" x 10½"

* 4 strips 4½" wide, cut into 10 rectangles 4½" x 10½"
* 3 strips 2⅜" wide, cut into 44 squares 2⅜" x 2⅜"
* 1 strip 4½" wide, cut into 4 squares 4½" x 4½"

Binding
* 6 strips 2¼" wide

Fusible Web
* 8 squares 10½" x 10½"
* 10 rectangles 4½" x 10½"

Making the Blocks

Step 1: Make an arc template (page 46).

Step 1

Step 2: Position the arc along the sides of 8 fusible web squares and 10 rectangles as shown. Trace the arc onto the fusible web.

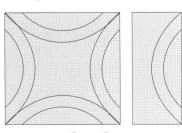

Step 2

Step 3: Fuse the traced squares and rectangles to the wrong side of the dark fabric. Use a sharp pair of scissors to cut **continuously** on the traced lines. Cut each square into 9 shapes and each rectangle into 3 shapes.

Step 3

Step 4: Arrange each set of shapes alternately on two background squares and fuse in place. Make a total of 15 square blocks—8 with light arcs and 7 with dark arcs. You'll have one extra set of dark arcs. Make a total of 16 rectangular blocks, 10 with dark arcs and 6 with light arcs. (You'll have 4 extra sets of shapes from the rectangles.)

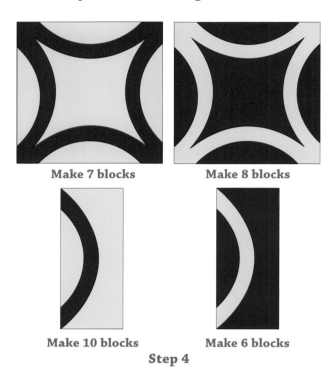

Make 7 blocks   Make 8 blocks

Make 10 blocks   Make 6 blocks

Step 4

Step 5: Use a zigzag or decorative stitch to sew the raw edges of the appliqué shapes.

Step 6: On the wrong side of each 2⅜" square, lightly mark a diagonal line from corner to corner. For both the square and rectangle blocks, pin the light squares to the corners of the dark-arc blocks and dark squares to the corners of light-arc blocks

as shown. Stitch on the marked line. Trim the seam allowance to ¼" and press the triangles toward the corners.

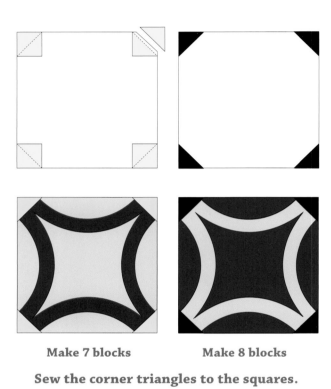

Make 7 blocks   Make 8 blocks

Sew the corner triangles to the squares.

Make 10 blocks   Make 6 blocks

Sew the corner triangles to the rectangles.

Step 6

Quilt assembly

Making the Quilt

Arrange the appliqué blocks, alternating the dark and light blocks. Position the appliquéd rectangles and corner squares around the edges. Sew the blocks into rows and join the rows. Press the seams open.

Sandwich the quilt top, batting, and backing, and baste well. Arlene quilted around each fused shape close to the appliqué stitching. She then quilted large curved motifs in the background of each square and rectangle and stippling in the rings.

Trim and bind the quilt.

I Do! I Do!

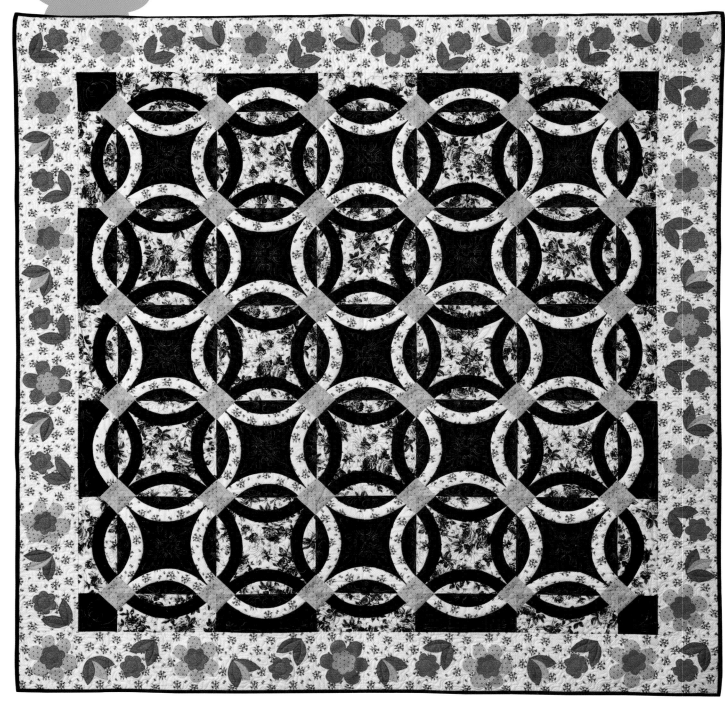

I Do! I Do!, 70" x 70", made by Susan Purney Mark, quilted by Phyllis Wright

Finished block size: 10" x 10", Number of blocks: 25

Materials

* Block background and inner border—black print on white background:

  large-scale print, 2 yards

  small-scale print, 2 yards
* Appliqué fabric, inner border, and binding— small-scale dark print, 2¾ yards
* Blocks and floral appliqué:

  light pink, ⅓ yards

  light green, 1 yard

* Floral Appliqué:

  dark pink, ½ yard

  dark green, ½ yard
* Outer Border—black print

  on white background, 2⅛ yards
* Backing, 4½ yards
* Batting, 78" x 78"
* Fusible Web, 6½ yards

Cutting Instructions

Cut all strips across the width of fabric unless otherwise noted.

Block background and inner border (light prints)

From the small-scale print:

* 6 strips 10½" wide, cut into 13 squares 10½" x 10½" and 8 rectangles 4½" x 10½"

From the large-scale print:

* 6 strips 10½" wide, cut into 12 squares 10½" x 10½" and 12 rectangles 4½" x 10½"

Block appliqué, inner border, and binding (dark print)

* 5 strips 10½" wide, cut into

  13 squares 10½" x 10½"
* 12 rectangles 4½" x 10½"
* 4 squares 4½" x 4½"

* 8 strips 2¼" wide

Outer border (cut lengthwise):

* 2 strips 6½" x 58½"
* 2 strips 6½" x 70½"

Light Pink

* 5 strips 2⅜" wide, cut into

  72 squares 2⅜" x 2⅜"

  Set the remainder aside for the appliqué.

Light Green

* 5 strips 2⅜" wide, cut into 72 squares 2⅜" x 2⅜"

  Set the remainder aside for the appliqué.

Fusible Web

* 13 squares 10½" x 10½"
* 12 rectangles 4½" x 10½"

  Set the remainder aside for the appliqué.

Making the Blocks

Step 1: Make an arc template (page 46).

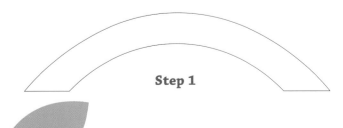

Step 1

Step 2: Position the arc along the sides of 13 fusible web squares and 12 rectangles as shown. Trace the arc onto the fusible web.

Step 2

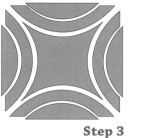 

Step 3

Step 3: Fuse the traced squares and rectangles to the wrong side of the dark fabric. Use a sharp pair of scissors to cut **continuously** on the traced lines. Cut each square into 9 shapes and each rectangle into 3 shapes.

Step 4: Arrange each set of shapes alternately on two background squares and fuse in place. Use the large scale print with the dark arcs to showcase the fabric. Make a total of 25 square blocks—13 with light arcs and 12 with dark arcs. You'll have one extra set of dark arcs. Make a total of 20 rectangular blocks, 12 with dark arcs and 8 with light arcs. (You'll have 4 extra sets of shapes from the rectangles.

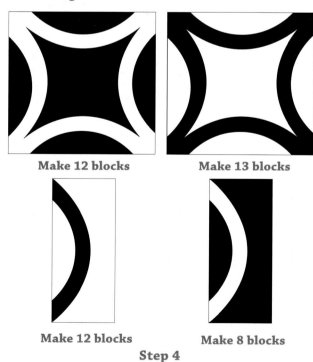

Make 12 blocks   **Make 13 blocks**

Make 12 blocks   **Make 8 blocks**

Step 4

Step 5: Use a zigzag or decorative stitch to sew the raw edges of the appliqué shapes.

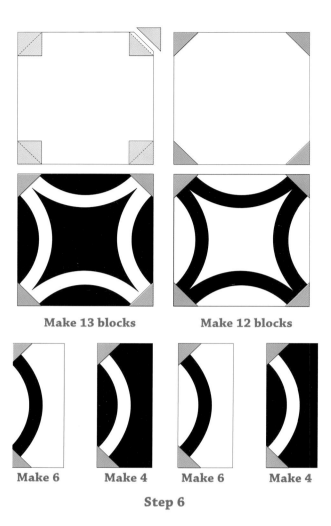

Make 13 blocks   **Make 12 blocks**

Make 6   **Make 4**   **Make 6**   **Make 4**

Step 6

Step 6: On the wrong side of each 2⅜" square, lightly mark a diagonal line from corner to corner. Pin squares to the corner of each appliquéd square. Pay close attention to the placement of the pink and green squares.

To ensure proper placement of the squares on the rectangle blocks, sort them into 2 piles, each with 6 rectangles with dark arcs and 4 with white arcs. On one pile, place the pink square at the top and the green square at the bottom. Reverse the placement on the rectangles in the second pile, as shown.

Stitch the squares on the marked line. Trim the seam allowance to ¼" and press the triangles toward the corners.

Making the Borders

Trace the flower and leaf shapes (page 47) onto the remainder of the fusible web and fuse to the wrong side of the appropriate fabrics. Cut along the marked lines. You will need:

Light Pink
* 14 large flowers
* 4 flower centers

Dark Pink
* 4 large flowers
* 32 small flowers

Light Green
* 16 leaves

Dark Green
* 68 leaves

Fold each cut border strip in half and press to mark the halfway point. Place the shapes evenly in a pleasing arrangement. Refer to the quilt photograph (page 42).

Use a zigzag or decorative stitch to sew the raw edges of the appliqué shapes. At the quilting stage, quilt stems to connect the flowers and leaves.

Making the Quilt

Arrange the appliqué blocks, alternating the dark and light arcs. Position the appliquéd rectangles and corner squares around the edges. Sew the blocks into rows and join the rows. Press the seams open. Add the appliquéd borders.

Sandwich the quilt top, batting, and backing, and baste well. Phyllis quilted an intricate looped design in the center of each appliquéd block and in the oval area at the block seams.

Trim and bind the quilt.

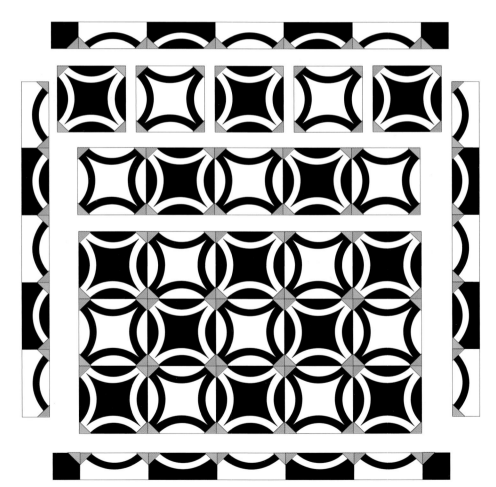

Quilt assembly

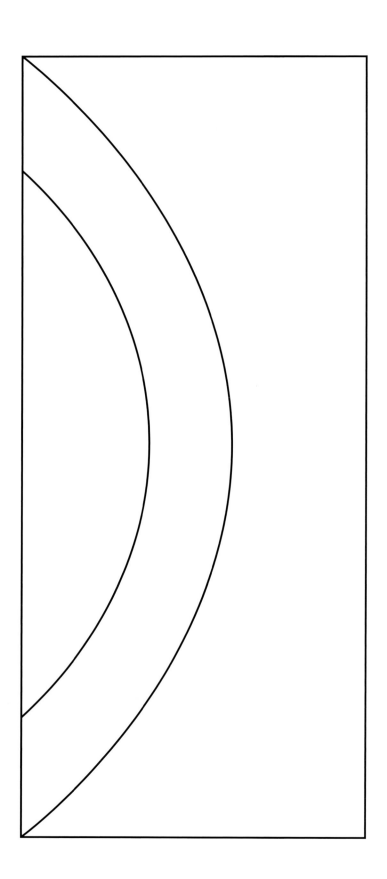

**Double Wedding Ring–
Appliqué template**

Enlarge pattern 125%

**Floral Appliqué templates–
for I Do! I Do!**

ORANGE PEEL PROJECTS

CHAPTER 6

ORANGE PEEL DESIGNS ARE USED BY CULTURES AROUND THE WORLD; WE OFTEN SEE THEM AS BORDER MOTIFS ON TEXTILES AND POTTERY AND THEY ARE COMMONLY FOUND ON JAPANESE DESIGNS IN SASHIKO EMBROIDERY AND INDIGO DYEING TECHNIQUES. TRY LOOKING AROUND AND YOU MIGHT FIND THE ORANGE PEEL DESIGN IN UNEXPECTED PLACES.

SUSAN CHOSE TO USE THE ORANGE PEEL MOTIF IN TWO DIFFERENT SHAPES, ONE SQUARE AND ONE A RECTANGLE. INTERESTING ILLUSIONS EMERGE WHEN QUILTERS PLAY WITH CHANGING THE SHAPES, AND SINCE THE MOTIFS FLOAT ON THE BACKGROUND, DIFFERENT SHAPES ARE NOT A PROBLEM.

COSMO CURVES, detail.
Full quilt on page 50.

COSMO CURVES is a contemporary design with strong bold shapes in an unusual layout. The color combination is a little different as well; the blue/greens set off with the charcoal grays offer a uniquely modern look. The checkerboard squares add interest and provide a frame effect to the blocks. The construction involves sewing partial seams in two areas, so pay careful attention to the instructions.

HOT TAMALES, was inspired by the Orange Peel shape that reminded Susan of a popular Hispanic dish of tamales, a rich mixture of cornmeal and meats wrapped in a corn husk for steaming. The background fabric in the outer blocks is cut to take advantage of the striped fabric. Stripes can add excitement and movement to a quilt so don't be nervous about using them. If you look for stripes in an uneven repeating pattern you won't have to worry about matching the design up at the seams. The strong pink diagonal sashing helps to tie the blocks together and placing the appliqué shapes in a different format shows that positive/negative repeats don't have to be sequential.

HOT TAMALES, detail.
Full quilt on page 54.

Cosmo Curves

COSMO CURVES, 48" x 33", made by Susan Purney Mark

Finished block size: 6" x 9"
Number of blocks: 24

....

Materials

* Block background and checkerboard squares—
  6 different light prints, ¼ yard EACH
  (1½ yards total)

* Block appliqué, checkerboard squares and
  binding—3 different dark prints, ½ yard EACH
  (1½ yards total)
* Backing, 1⅔ yards
* Batting, 56" x 41"
* Fusible Web, 2¼ yards

Cutting Instructions

Cut all strips across the width of fabric.

Block background (light prints)

* 1 strip 6½" wide from EACH of 6 fabrics, cut into 24 rectangles 6½" x 9½", 4 of EACH fabric
* 4 strips 2" wide from your choice of the fabrics

Block appliqué (dark prints)

* 1 strip 6½" wide from EACH of 3 fabrics cut into 12 rectangles 6½" x 9½", 4 of EACH fabric
* 4 strips 2" wide from your choice of fabrics
* 5 strips 2¼" wide for binding from your choice of fabric

Fusible Web

* 12 rectangles 6½" x 9½"

Making the Blocks

Step 1: Make an oval template (page 53).

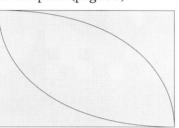

Step 2: Trace the oval onto the 12 fusible web rectangles.

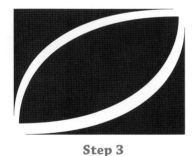

Step 3: Fuse the traced rectangles to the wrong side of the dark fabric. Use a sharp pair

Step 3

of scissors to cut **continuously** on the traced lines. Cut each rectangle into 3 shapes.

Step 4: Arrange each set of shapes alternately on two background rectangles and fuse in place. Make a total of 24 blocks.

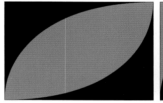

Step 4

Step 5: Use a zigzag or decorative stitch to sew the raw edges of the appliqué shapes.

Making the Checkerboard and Four-Patch Units

Make 4 strips-sets with the light and dark 2" strips. Press the seams open. Cut 64 segments 2" wide. Sew segments together into units as shown. Press the seams open.

Make 5   **Make 5**   **Make 2**

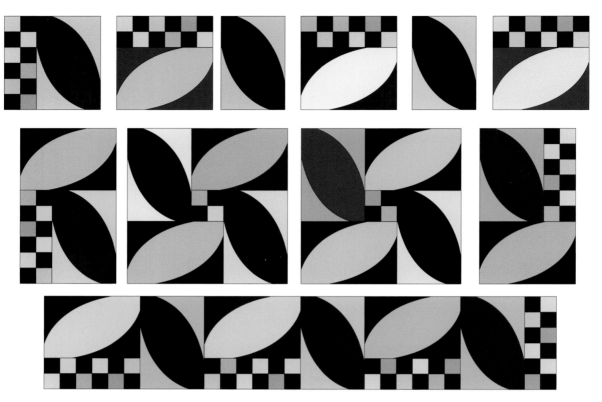

Quilt assembly

Making the Quilt

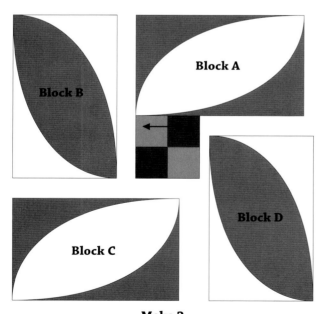

Make 2

Arrange 4 of the appliqué blocks and 1 four-patch unit as shown. Join Block A and the four-patch unit with a partial seam from Point A and following the

arrow. Press the partial seam toward the block. Add Block B, Block C, and Block D, pressing the seam toward the added block each time. Finish sewing and pressing the partial seam. Repeat to make one more unit.

Sew checkerboard units to 10 appliqué blocks as shown. Pay particular attention to the position of these units. Sew the units together in rows. Sew the rows together. Press the seams open.

Sandwich the quilt top, batting, and backing, and baste well. Susan quilted in the ditch around each block and around each fused shape close to the appliqué stitching. She then marked and quilted a feather swag in each oval and a small double swag over each checkerboard. Be sure to quilt evenly over the whole surface of your quilt.

Trim and bind the quilt.

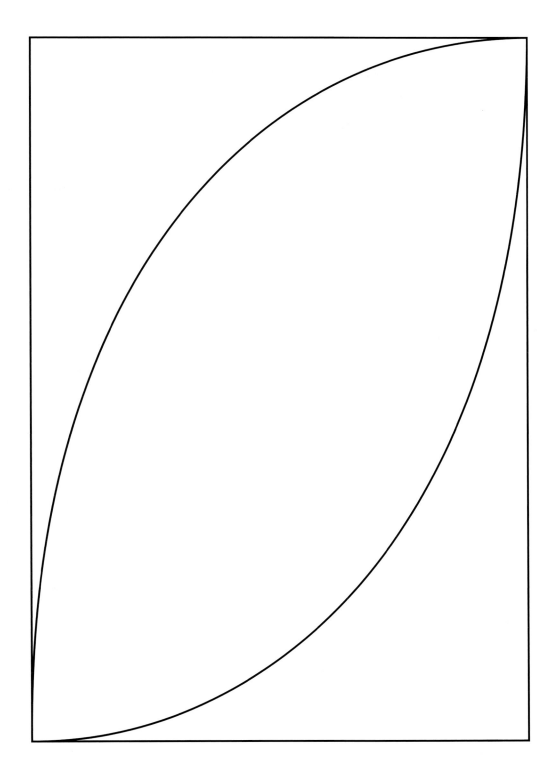

Appliqué template for COSMO CURVES

Enlarge pattern 125%

Hot Tamales

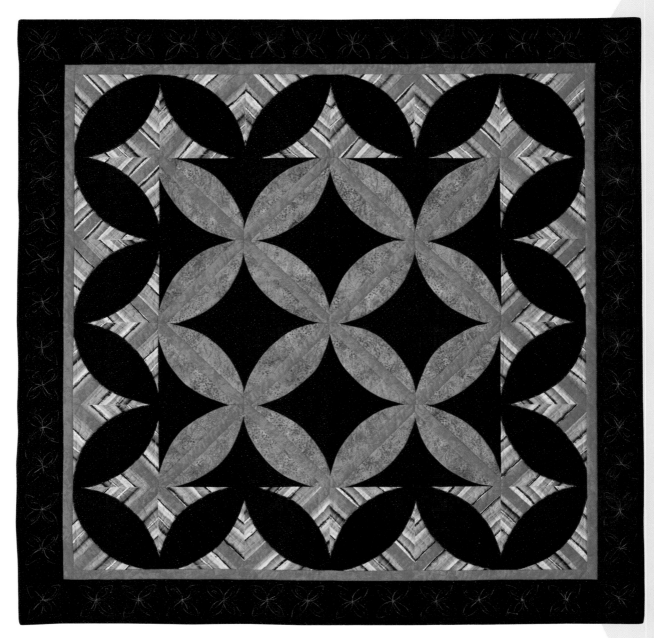

HOT TAMALES, 58" x 58", made by Susan Purney Mark

Finished block size: 8" x 8"
Number of blocks: 36

Materials

* Block background—
  pink print for inner blocks, ⅞ yard
* Block background—
  striped print for outer blocks, 1½ yards
* Inner border and diagonal sashing
  for blocks, 1 yard
* Block appliqué, border, and binding—
  dark print, 2½ yards
* Backing, 3⅞ yards
* Batting, 66" x 66"
* Fusible Web, 5 yards

Cutting Instructions

Cut all strips across the width of fabric.

Block background (pink print)

Cut 32 triangles

* 4 strips 7" wide, cut into 16 squares 7" x 7".
  Cut each square in half diagonally.

Block background (striped print)

Cut 40 triangles

* 8 strips 6" wide, EACH cut into 5 triangles
  Use the 45-degree line on your rotary ruler
  as shown. Cut a total of 40 triangles.

Diagonal sashing for blocks and inner border

* 19 strips, 1½" wide
  Set 6 strips aside for the inner border.

Block appliqué, border, and binding (dark print)

* 5 strips 8½" wide, cut into 20 squares for blocks
* 6 strips 4½" wide for border
* 6 strips 2¼" wide for binding

Fusible Web

* 20 squares, 8½" x 8½"

Making the Blocks

Step 1: Sew 20 striped triangles to the 1½" strips, spacing them 2" apart on the strip and leaving 1" of the strip before the first triangle and at least 1" of the strip after the last triangle. Press the seams open. Cut the triangles apart, leaving 1" of the attached strip at each end.

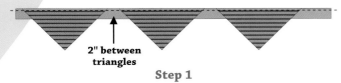

2" between triangles

Step 1

Step 2: Center a second triangle on top of each triangle/strip unit, right sides together, matching the long raw edges. Sew with a ¼" seam and press the seams open.

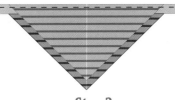

Step 2

Step 3: Trim blocks to measure 8½" x 8½", centering the sashing strip diagonally in the middle of the squares. Make 20 striped background blocks.

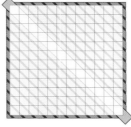

Step 3

Step 4: Repeat these steps with the print triangles. Make 16 print background blocks.

Step 5: Trace the oval (page 57) onto the 20 squares of fusible web.

Step 5

Fuse the traced squares to the wrong side of the dark fabric squares. Use a sharp pair of scissors to cut **continuously** on the traced lines. Cut each square into 3 shapes.

Step 6: Arrange the shapes on background squares and fuse in place. (There will be 8 leftover "outside" shapes.)

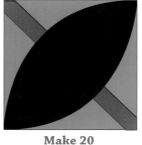
Make 20

Make 16

Step 6

Step 7: Use a zigzag or decorative stitch to appliqué the shapes.

Making the Quilt

Arrange the appliqué blocks as shown. Sew the blocks into rows and sew the rows together. Press the seams open.

Add the inner border using the 1½" wide strips.

Add the outer border using the 4½" wide strips.

Sandwich the quilt top, batting, and backing and baste well. Susan quilted in the ditch around each block and around each fused shape close to the appliqué stitching. She repeated the Orange Peel motif in the outer borders.

Trim and bind the quilt.

Quilt assembly

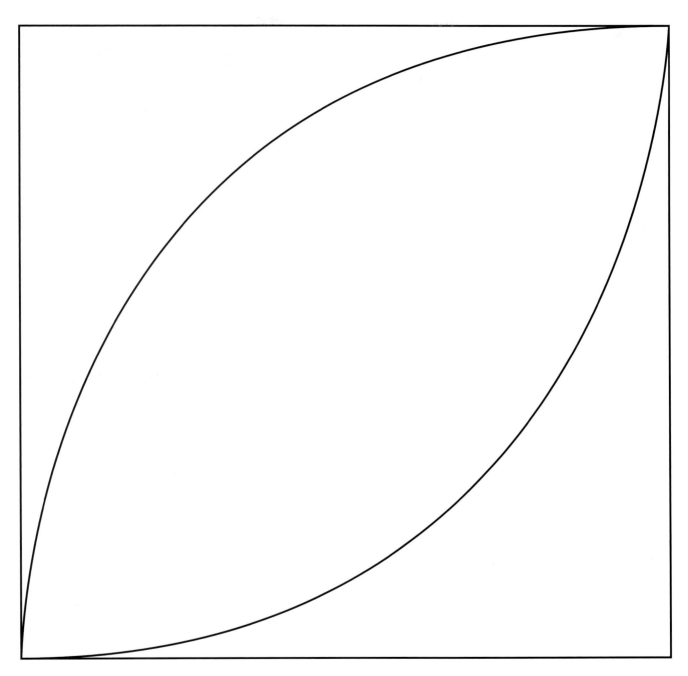

Appliqué template for HOT TAMALES

Enlarge pattern 125%

CHAPTER 7

PICKLE DISH PROJECTS

The two projects in this chapter are inspired by a traditional Pickle Dish block. Smooth curves and sharp points are the most important elements of this block. It is easy to achieve both with Give and Take Appliqué.

Fabric choices for both projects are wide-ranging. The mood of your quilt can be changed simply by selecting different fabrics. The fabrics for both quilts were selected after the border fabrics were chosen. This is a common way to build a palette of fabrics for a project. The staff at your local quilt shop will be happy to help you select fabrics to go with the border fabric you choose.

Grandma's Pawpaws, detail.
Full quilt on page 60.

The Grandma's Pawpaws quilt uses soft colors; however, there is high contrast between the two fabrics used in each block. The variety of print sizes adds more interest to the quilt. The fabrics in this quilt remind us of a well-loved quilt, soft, cuddly, perhaps one made by a dear grandma.

Sweet Mixed Pickles uses bold colors and the block arrangement results in a more contemporary design. The result is a strong wallhanging that would make a statement in any room. When choosing fabrics for the appliqué, Daphne wanted the subtle textures of tone-on-tone fabrics. Three colors seemed appropriate and worked well with the border fabric. Wanting more variety, she chose two prints in each color. Many fabric companies produce lines of basic or blender fabrics; this is a great place to look for fabrics for this quilt.

The quilts use the same number of Pickle Dish blocks but the different fabrics, two block sizes, and arrangements produce two very different quilts.

Sweet Mixed Pickles, detail.
Full quilt on page 64.

Grandma's Pawpaws

GRANDMA'S PAWPAWS, 47" x 63", made by Daphne Greig

Finished block size: 6" x 6"

Number of blocks: 24

Materials

* Block background—light print, 1 yard
* Block appliqué—
  dark print #1, ½ yard
  dark print #2, ¼ yard
* Alternate squares—medium print, ¾ yard

* Inner border, ⅜ yard
* Setting triangles, outer border,
  and binding, 2 yards
* Backing (pieced crosswise), 3¼ yards
* Batting, 55" x 71"
* Fusible Web, 2¼ yards

Cutting Instructions

Cut all strips across the width of fabric unless otherwise noted.

Block background (light print)
* 4 strips 6½" wide, cut into 24 squares 6½" x 6½"

Block appliqué (dark print #1)
* 2 strips 6½" wide, cut into 8 squares 6½" x 6½"

Block appliqué (dark print #2)
* 1 strip 6½" wide, cut into 4 squares 6½" x 6½"

Alternate squares (medium print)
* 3 strips 6½" wide, cut into 15 squares 6½" x 6½"

Inner border
* 7 strips 1½" wide

Setting triangles, outer border and binding

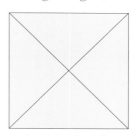

Cut 16 triangles

* 1 strip 9¾" wide, cut into 4 squares 9¾" x 9¾"; cut each square into quarters

* 1 strip 5⅛" wide, cut into 2 squares; cut each square in half diagonally (4 triangles total)

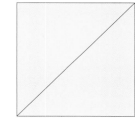

* From the remaining fabric cut four 6" strips LENGTHWISE for the outer border.

* Use the rest of the fabric to cut 2¼" strips for binding. You will need a total of 242" for the binding.

Fusible Web
* 12 squares 6½" x 6½"

Making the Blocks

Step 1: Trace 12 patterns onto the 6½" squares of fusible web.

Step 2: Fuse the traced squares to the wrong side of the 2 different dark print squares—8 of one fabric and 4 of the other.

Use a sharp pair of scissors to cut **continuously** on the traced lines. Cut each fused fabric square into 6 shapes.

Step 2

Step 3: Arrange each set of shapes alternately on two background squares and fuse in place. Make 24 blocks.

Step 4: Use a zigzag or decorative stitch to sew the raw edges of the appliqué shapes.

Step 3

Making the Quilt

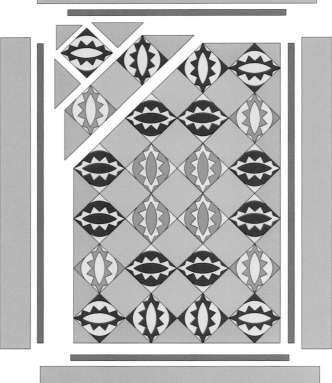

Quilt assembly

Arrange the appliqué blocks, alternate medium squares, and setting triangles in diagonal rows as shown. Sew the units into diagonal rows. Press the seam allowances away from the appliqué blocks. Sew the rows together. Press the seams open.

Add the inner border using the 1½" wide strips.

Add the outer border using the 6" wide strips.

Sandwich the quilt top, batting, and backing and baste well. Daphne quilted in the ditch around each block and around each fused shape close to the appliqué stitching. She marked and quilted a large motif in the alternate squares and part of the same motif in the setting and corner triangles. Straight lines, ¼" from the seams, were quilted in the inner border and the outer border has a freeform feather design.

Trim and bind the quilt.

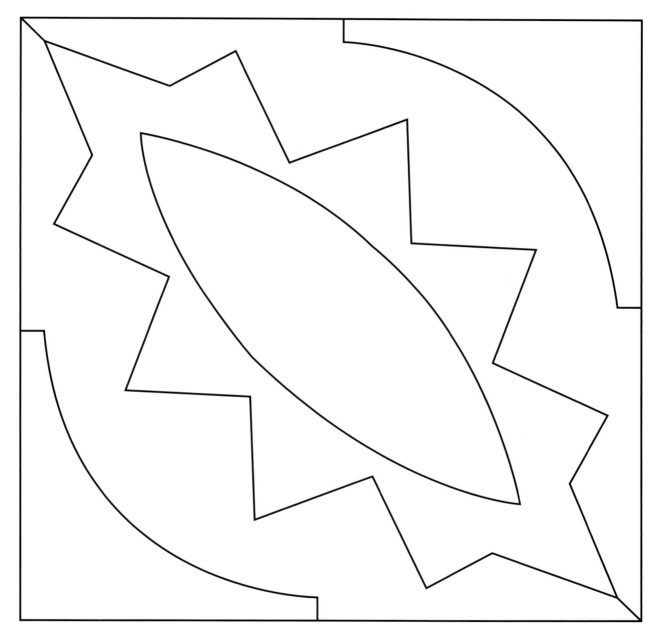

**Appliqué template for GRANDMA'S PAWPAWS—
6½" unfinished block**

Sweet Mixed Pickles

SWEET MIXED PICKLES, 42" x 54", made by Daphne Greig

Finished block size: 7" x 7", Number of blocks: 24

Materials

* Block background—light print, 1¼ yards
* Pickle Fabrics—dark prints: 6 fabrics, 2 EACH of 3 colors; ¼ yard or 1 fat quarter of EACH fabric

* Sashing—very dark solid or tone-on-tone, ½ yard
* Outer border and binding, 1¾ yards
* Backing (pieced crosswise), 3 yards
* Batting, 50" x 62"
* Fusible Web, 2¾ yards

Cutting Instructions

Cut all strips across the width of fabric unless otherwise noted.

Block background (light print)
* 5 strips 7½" wide, cut into 24 squares 7½" x 7½"

Block appliqué (dark prints)
* 2 squares 7½" x 7½" from EACH fabric, for a total of 12 squares

Sashing
* 5 strips 2¼" wide

Outer border and binding
* 2 strips 4¾" wide for the top and bottom borders.

* From the remaining fabric, cut 2 strips 4¾" LENGTHWISE for the side borders.

* Use the rest of the fabric to cut 2¼" strips for binding. You will need approximately 200" for the binding.

Fusible Web
* 12 squares 7½" x 7½"

Making the Blocks

Step 1: Trace 12 patterns onto the 7½" squares of fusible web.

Step 2: Fuse the traced squares to the wrong side of the dark appliqué fabric squares—2 of each fabric. Use a sharp pair of scissors to cut **continuously** on the traced lines. Cut each fused fabric square into 6 shapes.

Step 2

Step 3: Arrange a set of shapes alternately on two background squares and fuse in place. Repeat to make 24 blocks.

Step 3

Step 4: Use a zigzag or decorative stitch to sew the raw edges of the appliqué shapes.

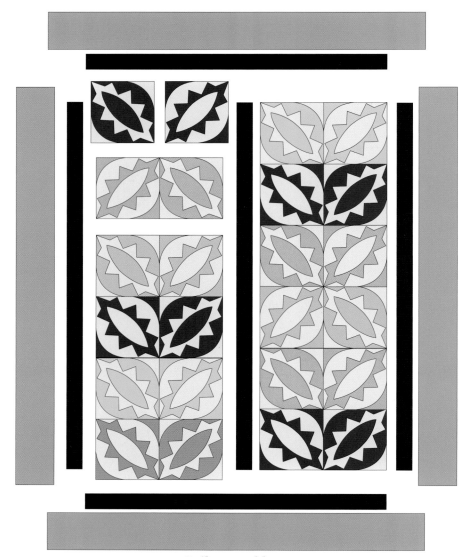

Quilt assembly

Making the Quilt

Arrange the appliqué blocks in 4 vertical rows of 6 blocks each as shown. Sew horizontal pairs of blocks together and press seams open. Then sew the pairs together into two units. Press the seams open.

Measure the length of the block units and cut 3 sashing strips 2¼" wide to match. Add to the units and press the seams toward the sashing.

Measure the width and add sashing strips to the top and bottom. Press as before.

Add the outer border using the 4¾" wide strips. Press the seams toward the border.

Sandwich the quilt top, batting, and backing and baste well. Daphne quilted around each fused shape, close to the appliqué stitching, and in the ditch around the sashing. To add more interest to the sashing strips, she stitched a decorative blanket stitch on the sashing strips using a heavy 40-wt thread. Finally, she marked and quilted a motif based on the center of the appliqué block in the outer border.

Trim and bind the quilt.

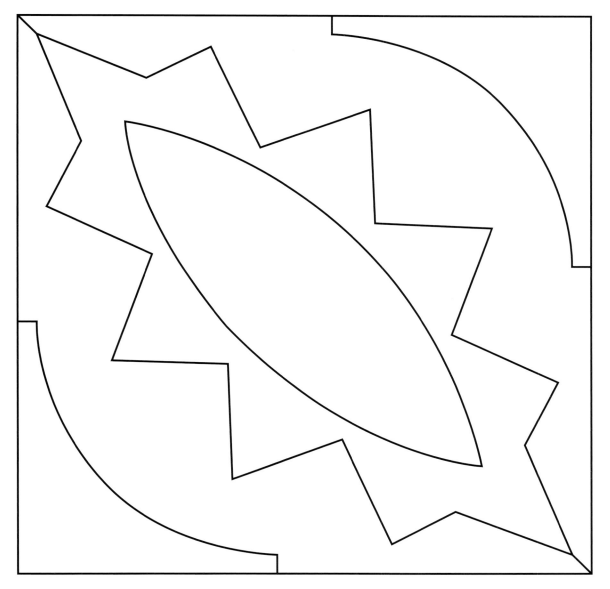

Appliqué template for SWEET MIXED PICKLES—
7½" unfinished block
Enlarge pattern 125%

CHAPTER 8
FANCY FANS PROJECTS

If you are familiar with a traditional Drunkard's Path block, you know that there are unlimited layout options for the quarter-circle design. The key element is the contrast of light and dark in the blocks, providing both visual interest and shape to the design.

Susan chose to delve into her scrap bag (and make a couple of trips to her local quilt shop) for the fabrics for these two quilts. She wanted to have a "juicy" assortment of yellows, oranges, and reds to make her mouth water for Citrus Salad. A stack of fat quarters was the perfect solution— already preselected and tied with a pretty ribbon. Susan also used the fat quarters for the borders. Since they were too short for the sides, she pieced them and used different fabrics for each one. Using the leftover fabrics for a pieced backing meant she got maximum value from that pack of fat quarters.

Citrus Salad, detail.
Full quilt on page 70.

Ball Joints uses the quarter-circle design again, but this time Susan added spikes and circles, hence the name of the quilt. In this quilt, color plays a more secondary role to value, but Susan chose the theme of dots and circles from her scrap collection. It seemed like a perfect fit! The border treatment continues the checkerboard design and gives a cohesive look to the quilt. Quilters can choose to eliminate the border or use only one fabric.

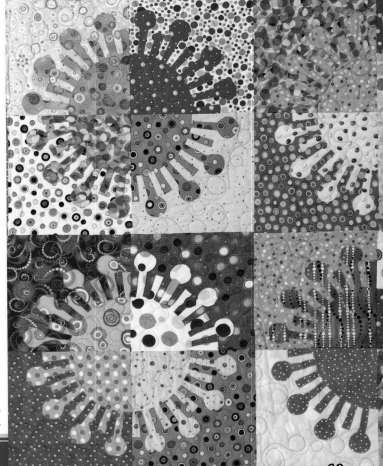

Ball Joints, detail.
Full quilt on page 74.

Citrus Salad

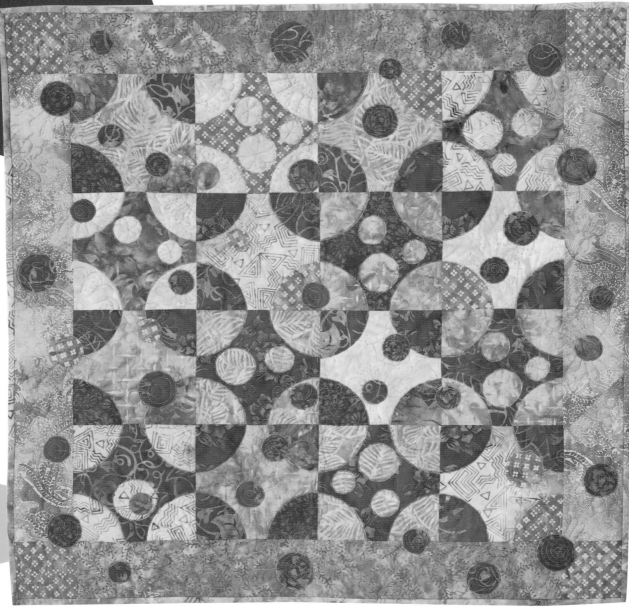

CITRUS SALAD, 35" x 35", made by Susan Purney Mark

Finished block size: 7" x 7"

Number of blocks: 16

Materials

* Block background—a variety of light prints to total 1 yard

* Appliqué fabrics—a variety of dark prints to total ½ yard

* Border fabrics—two fabrics, ¼ yard EACH

* Border cornerstones, ¼ yard

* Binding, ½ yard

* Backing, 1¼ yards

* Batting, 39" x 39"

* Fusible web, 1½ yards

Cutting Instructions

Cut all strips across the width of fabric.

Block background (light prints)
* 16 squares 7½" x 7½"

Block appliqué (dark prints)
* 8 squares 7½" x 7½"

Border fabrics
* 2 strips 4" of EACH fabric

Border cornerstones
* 4 squares 4" x 4"

Binding
* 5 strips 2¼"

Fusible Web
* 8 squares 6½" x 6½"

Making the Blocks

Step 1: Trace the design onto 8 fusible web squares. Trace only one or two of the inner circles on some of the squares. The quilt is more visually interesting when each block is slightly different from its neighbors. Refer to the quilt photograph. Fuse the traced squares to the wrong side of the dark fabric squares.

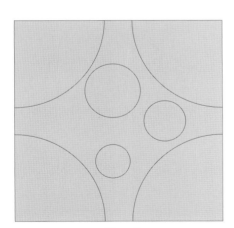

Step 1

Step 2: Use a sharp pair of scissors to cut **continuously** on the traced lines. You will have five shapes from each fused square plus the number of inner circles that you have chosen to trace. Set aside the small circles to be fused when the quilt top is assembled.

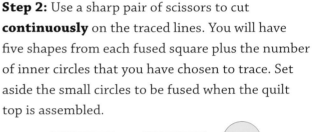
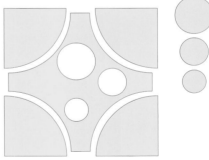

Step 2

Step 3: Arrange the appliqué shapes randomly on the background squares and fuse in place. Make a total of 16 blocks.

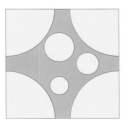

Make 16

Step 3

Step 4: Use a zigzag or decorative stitch to sew the raw edges of the appliqué shapes.

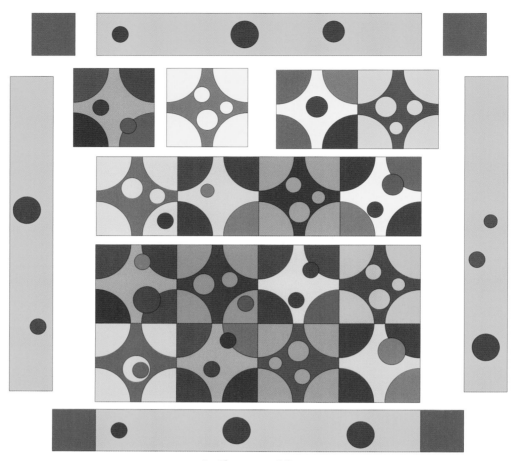

Quilt assembly

Making the Quilt

Arrange the appliqué blocks in 4 rows of 4 blocks each. Sew the blocks into rows and press the seams open. Sew the rows together and press the seams open.

Measure the length and width of the quilt top. The measurements should be the same. Cut 4 borders from the 4" wide strips to match that measurement. Add the side borders. Press the seams toward the borders. Sew 2 cornerstones to the ends of the top and bottom border strips and add them to the quilt. Press as before.

Arrange the remaining circles randomly over the quilt top; refer to the quilt photograph. Use an appliqué pressing sheet and fuse the circles in place. Appliqué each circle in place.

Sandwich the quilt top, batting, and backing and baste well. Susan quilted in the ditch around each block and around each fused shape close to the appliqué stitching, then quilted a variety of different sized circles using contrasting threads.

Trim and bind the quilt.

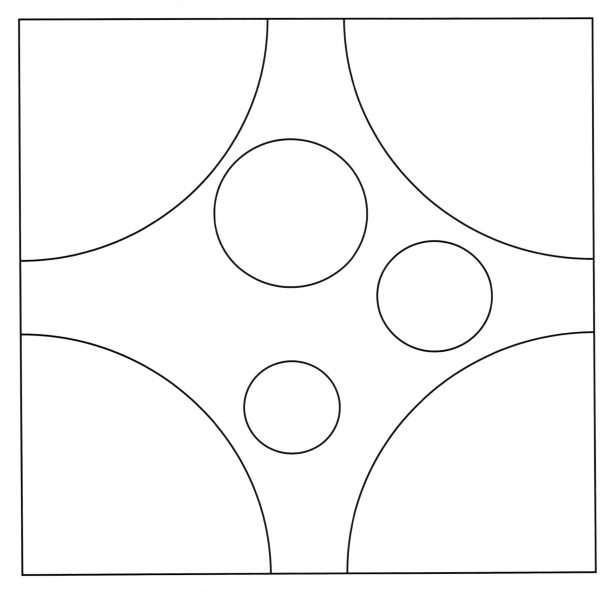

Appliqué template for CITRUS SALAD—
7½" unfinished block

Enlarge pattern 125%

Ball Joints

BALL JOINTS, 72" x 72", made by Susan Purney Mark, quilted by Arlene Mackenzie

Finished block size: 8" x 8", Number of blocks: 64

Materials

* Block background—a variety of light prints to total 4¾ yards
* Block appliqué—a variety of dark prints to total 2¾ yards
* Binding, ⅝ yard
* Backing (pieced crosswise), 4¾ yards
* Batting, 80" x 80"
* Fusible web, 7¾ yards

Cutting Instructions

Cut all strips across the width of fabric.

Block background (light prints)
* 16 strips 8½" wide, cut into 64 squares 8½" x 8½"
* 5 strips 4½" wide, cut into 16 rectangles 4½" x 8½" and 2 squares 4½" x 4½"

Block appliqué (dark prints)
* 8 strips 8½" wide, cut into 32 squares 8½" x 8½"
* 5 strips 4½" wide, cut into 16 rectangles 4½" x 8½" and 2 squares 4½" x 4½"

Binding
* 8 strips 2¼" wide

Fusible Web
* 32 squares 8½" x 8½"

Making the Blocks

Step 1: Trace the design onto 32 fusible web squares. Fuse the traced squares to the wrong side of the dark fabric squares.

Step 1

Step 2: Use a sharp pair of scissors to cut **continuously** on the traced lines. You will have 2 shapes cut from each fused dark square.

Step 2

Step 3: Pay attention to value when placing the appliqué on the background squares. Fuse the appliqué shapes in place. Make 64 blocks.

Step 3

Step 4: Use a zigzag or decorative stitch to sew the raw edges of the appliqué shapes.

Making the Quilt

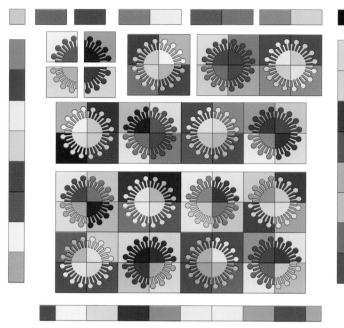

Quilt assembly

Add 2 strips to the sides, paying attention to the placement of the lights and darks. Press the seam allowances toward the borders. Add cornerstones to the remaining 2 border strips and add to the top and bottom of the quilt. Press as before.

Sandwich the quilt top, batting, and backing and baste well. Arlene quilted a large loopy design over the entire quilt. Susan then stitched around each shape with invisible thread, close to the appliqué, to help define the shapes.

Trim and bind the quilt.

Arrange the appliqué blocks in 8 rows with 8 blocks in each row as shown or try an alternate arrangement. Sew the blocks into rows. Press the seam allowances open. Sew the rows together. Press the seams open.

Sew the 4½" x 8½" dark rectangles into pairs, repeat for the 4½" x 8½" light rectangles. Sew 4 pairs together end-to-end, alternating dark and light pairs. Repeat to make 4 border strips.

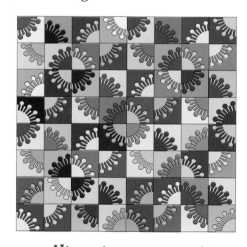

Alternate arrangements

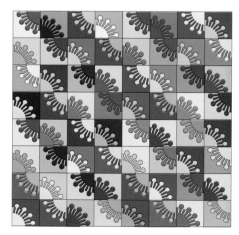

Appliqué template for BALL JOINTS

Enlarge pattern 125%

RESOURCES

Daphne and Susan

are available for teaching and lecturing engagements.

DAPHNE GREIG
www.daphnegreig.com
email: info@daphnegreig.com

SUSAN PURNEY MARK
www.susanpm.com
email: patchworkstudio@shaw.ca

Daphne & Susan's books & patterns are available at www.patchworkstudio.com

QUILT UNIVERSITY
Online quilting courses
www.quiltuniversity.com

Fabrics

NORTHCOTT/LYNDHURST
www.northcott.net
phone: (800) 268-1466

MODA FABRICS
www.unitednotions.com
phone: (800) 527-9447

FINE LINES FABRIC
www.finelinesfabric.com
phone (319) 895-8063

Tools & Supplies

LITE STEAM-A-SEAM 2®
THE WARM COMPANY
www.warmcompany.com
phone: (425) 248-2424

Thread

SUPERIOR THREADS
www.superiorthreads.com
phone: (800) 499-1777

Longarm Quilting Services

ARLENE MacKENZIE,
ON POINT QUILTING STUDIO
www.onpointquiltingstudio.com
North Saanich, BC Canada

PHYLLIS WRIGHT,
QUILTING SEW FINE
Victoria, BC Canada
phone: (250) 727-9672

About the Authors

Daphne Greig & Susan Purney Mark

Daphne can't remember a time when she wasn't creating with fabric, fiber, or thread. She began sewing as a young girl, making outfits for her dolls. Her first teacher was her mother, an experienced sewer and embroiderer. Daphne sewed garments and enjoyed knitting and several forms of embroidery until she discovered her passion for quilting in 1984. She has been teaching quiltmaking classes for over 20 years. Her work has been exhibited in Canada and the United States, and she travels internationally presenting lectures and workshops for shops, guilds, and major quilting events. Daphne regularly writes articles for several quilting magazines and teaches online workshops through Quilt University. Together with Susan Purney Mark she owns Patchworks Studio, a pattern design company. They have also co-authored four books.

Daphne continually expands her quilting and fiber art skills by experimenting with new techniques in her home studio in North Saanich, British Columbia. She and her husband, Alan, enjoy golfing, gardening, and travel. Further information about Daphne's lectures and workshops can be found on her website, www.daphnegreig.com.

Susan's quilting journey began almost 30 years ago and has continued unabated, with enthusiasm building over the years. Quilts of all shapes, sizes, and colors have poured out of her studio yet her stash of fabric continues to grow! Her interests include quilting history, design, and techniques. She also works with surface design, dyeing, painting, and embellishments. Susan writes for several quilt magazines and teaches online at Quilt University. She has exhibited in Canada and the United States and she is available to teach for quilt guilds, shops, and conferences.

In 1996 she formed a quilt pattern company, Patchworks Studio, (www.patchworkstudio.com) with Daphne. They have created dozens of patterns, an online quilt series, and have co-authored three books with AQS—*Quilted Havens: City Houses*, *Country Homes* (1999), *Fat Quarter Frenzy* (2005), and *Fat Quarter Frenzy Two* (2008). They continue to collaborate on many of their designs and publishing work.

Susan lives in Victoria, British Columbia, with her husband, Henry, where they enjoy gardening, hiking, and camping. She invites you to visit her website at www.susanpm.com.

more AQS Books

This is only a small selection of the books available from the American Quilter's Society. AQS books are known worldwide for timely topics, clear writing, beautiful color photos, and accurate illustrations and patterns. The following books are available from your local bookseller, quilt shop, or public library.

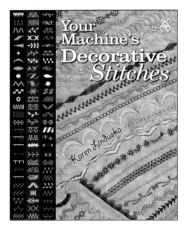

#8353

#8356

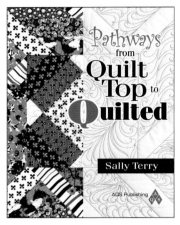

#8348

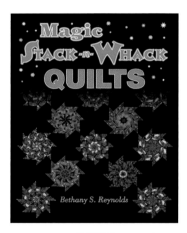

#4995

#8240

#8355

#8349

#8238

#8347

LOOK for these books nationally.
CALL or **VISIT** our website at

1-800-626-5420
www.AmericanQuilter.com